I0420278

THE THREAT OF ISLAMIC EXTREMISM IN RUSSIA

HEARING

BEFORE THE

SUBCOMMITTEE ON EUROPE, EURASIA, AND
EMERGING THREATS

OF THE

COMMITTEE ON FOREIGN AFFAIRS
HOUSE OF REPRESENTATIVES

ONE HUNDRED FOURTEENTH CONGRESS

FIRST SESSION

SEPTEMBER 30, 2015

Serial No. 114–98

Printed for the use of the Committee on Foreign Affairs

Available via the World Wide Web: http://www.foreignaffairs.house.gov/ or
http://www.gpo.gov/fdsys/

U.S. GOVERNMENT PUBLISHING OFFICE

96–819PDF   WASHINGTON : 2015

For sale by the Superintendent of Documents, U.S. Government Publishing Office
Internet: bookstore.gpo.gov   Phone: toll free (866) 512–1800; DC area (202) 512–1800
Fax: (202) 512–2104   Mail: Stop IDCC, Washington, DC 20402–0001

COMMITTEE ON FOREIGN AFFAIRS

EDWARD R. ROYCE, California, *Chairman*

CHRISTOPHER H. SMITH, New Jersey
ILEANA ROS-LEHTINEN, Florida
DANA ROHRABACHER, California
STEVE CHABOT, Ohio
JOE WILSON, South Carolina
MICHAEL T. McCAUL, Texas
TED POE, Texas
MATT SALMON, Arizona
DARRELL E. ISSA, California
TOM MARINO, Pennsylvania
JEFF DUNCAN, South Carolina
MO BROOKS, Alabama
PAUL COOK, California
RANDY K. WEBER SR., Texas
SCOTT PERRY, Pennsylvania
RON DeSANTIS, Florida
MARK MEADOWS, North Carolina
TED S. YOHO, Florida
CURT CLAWSON, Florida
SCOTT DesJARLAIS, Tennessee
REID J. RIBBLE, Wisconsin
DAVID A. TROTT, Michigan
LEE M. ZELDIN, New York
DANIEL DONOVAN, New York

ELIOT L. ENGEL, New York
BRAD SHERMAN, California
GREGORY W. MEEKS, New York
ALBIO SIRES, New Jersey
GERALD E. CONNOLLY, Virginia
THEODORE E. DEUTCH, Florida
BRIAN HIGGINS, New York
KAREN BASS, California
WILLIAM KEATING, Massachusetts
DAVID CICILLINE, Rhode Island
ALAN GRAYSON, Florida
AMI BERA, California
ALAN S. LOWENTHAL, California
GRACE MENG, New York
LOIS FRANKEL, Florida
TULSI GABBARD, Hawaii
JOAQUIN CASTRO, Texas
ROBIN L. KELLY, Illinois
BRENDAN F. BOYLE, Pennsylvania

AMY PORTER, *Chief of Staff*   THOMAS SHEEHY, *Staff Director*
JASON STEINBAUM, *Democratic Staff Director*

————

SUBCOMMITTEE ON EUROPE, EURASIA, AND EMERGING THREATS

DANA ROHRABACHER, California, *Chairman*

TED POE, Texas
TOM MARINO, Pennsylvania
MO BROOKS, Alabama
PAUL COOK, California
RANDY K. WEBER SR., Texas
REID J. RIBBLE, Wisconsin
DAVID A. TROTT, Michigan

GREGORY W. MEEKS, New York
ALBIO SIRES, New Jersey
THEODORE E. DEUTCH, Florida
WILLIAM KEATING, Massachusetts
LOIS FRANKEL, Florida
TULSI GABBARD, Hawaii

CONTENTS

THE THREAT OF ISLAMIC EXTREMISM IN RUSSIA

WEDNESDAY, SEPTEMBER 30, 2015

House of Representatives,
Subcommittee on Europe, Eurasia, and Emerging Threats,
Committee on Foreign Affairs,
Washington, DC.

The subcommittee met, pursuant to notice, at 2 o'clock p.m., in room 2200, Rayburn House Office Building, Hon. Dana Rohrabacher (chairman of the subcommittee) presiding.

Mr. ROHRABACHER. We call to order this hearing of the Europe, Eurasia, and Emerging Threats Subcommittee.

This afternoon we will hear testimony, expert testimony, on the topic not thought to be, but in reality of great concern and importance, the threat of Islamic extremism inside Russia and what that might mean to the United States and global security.

The fight against violent, radical Islam is one of the major challenges of our time. Islamic terrorists have targeted numerous countries for attack, including the United States and Russia. They have declared war on the modern civilized world. Their barbaric actions in Syria remind us daily of their depravity. They must be stopped and they must be defeated. The future of America, Russia, and, yes, of Western civilization, depends on that. The lives of millions will be in jeopardy if we don't do what is right today.

Given the global nature of this fight, it is in the interests of our national interests to understand the growth of extremism in other parts of the world and in other countries, such as Russia. It is alarming to read reports of Muslims living in peaceful and in free democratic countries being attracted or recruited into radical Islamic terrorism. This frightening reality is happening in Europe and elsewhere. Media reports indicate that over 2,000 Russian-born fighters may have traveled to the Middle East to join ISIL. Our collective inability to stem this tide is both shocking and unnerving.

This afternoon, I look forward to hearing from all of our witnesses. I know Dr. Aron we are pleased to welcome back as a witness, has some unique insights regarding the spread of extremism into Muslim populations inside Russia. We don't normally associate this behavior with such Russian ethnic groups, like the Tatars or others, but we need to know what those details are. We will learn more about this and other things in your testimony.

And also, in the aftermath of the Boston bombing in May 2013, I led a congressional delegation to Russia where we met with Russian Government and intelligence officials and discussed the threat

(1)

of terrorism and how our governments could potentially cooperate. I have been disappointed that, due to the upheaval in Ukraine, more has not been achieved in implementing cooperation in this area.

Of course, extremist forces continue to plot attacks against both the United States and Russia. It seems plain to me that if we work together we will be better able to protect our people, stop attacks, and kill violent terrorists—something I am personally in favor of as a matter of policy.

Please let me note our discussion today about Russia and the question of finding possible areas of cooperation in no way downplays or overlooks the disappointing situation in Ukraine. As a result, our government has imposed sanctions on Russian officials and institutions. Even with that millstone around our necks, our two governments still manage to achieve an admirable level of cooperation in other areas, like the International Space Station, for example. Perhaps our governments might also make a joint effort to stop the spread of Islamic extremism and the terrorism that flows from it.

Without objection, all members will have 5 legislative days to submit written questions or extraneous materials for the record.

And I will introduce the witnesses after opening statements from Mr. Sires and our colleagues.

Mr. SIRES. Thank you, Mr. Chairman, for holding today's timely hearing on Russia and the Islamic extremists.

Since coming into power 15 years ago, Vladimir Putin has been committed to restoring Russia as a great power, shaping his policy to position Russia as a counterweight to the United States. We saw Putin flex his muscles in the annexation of Crimea last year and the subsequent fighting in Ukraine. Now Russia has shifted its attention to increased support for the Assad regime and an increased role in the Syrian conflict.

At the U.N. this week, Putin continued his talk of the importance of mounting a broad effort to support Assad as the only way to fight against the spread of the Islamic State. Russia's plan to combat Islamic extremists through the support of Assad and to strengthen its military presence in Syria directly contradicts with the U.S. diplomatic goals to have Assad transition out of power.

It is unclear whether Putin's motives in Syria and the Middle East are self-serving or stem from the growing concern over a large number of jihadist fighters from the North Caucasus fighting in Syria who could pose a serious problem for Moscow should they return to Russia.

Given that the U.S. and Russia are at a critical crossroads in conversations on how to best combat Islamic extremists, I look forward to hearing from our esteemed panel of witnesses on the possible outcomes and solutions to the current challenges.

Thank you, Mr. Chairman.

Mr. ROHRABACHER. Thank you.

Mr. Brooks has no opening statement, but how about Mr. Weber? Do you have a short opening statement?

Mr. WEBER. Yeah. Welcome. Let's go.

Mr. ROHRABACHER. He is great. All right.

With that said, I will ask the witnesses to summarize your prepared statements. Hopefully, they are 5-minute summaries, and then we can have a dialogue and have some questions and answers. First, I am going to introduce all of the witnesses, and then we will proceed.

Dr. Leon Aron is a resident scholar and director of Russian Studies at the American Enterprise Institute. Starting this year, he joined the Broadcasting Board of Governors, the organization which oversees operations of international broadcasting, such as Voice of America. He is a widely published author and has earned his Ph.D. at Columbia University.

Simon Saradzhyan is a research fellow at the Kennedy School, Belfer Center for Science and International Affairs at Harvard University. He is also the assistant director of the U.S.-Russia Initiative to Prevent Nuclear Terrorism. Prior, he worked as a journalist in Russia for 15 years, where he covered several major events, including the terrorist attack at Beslan.

Next, we have Dr. Mark Katz, who is a professor of government and politics at George Mason University. He has authored many books and articles, for example, ''Leaving Without Losing: The War on Terror After Iraq and Afghanistan.'' Very fascinating. Thank you. He earned his Ph.D. from the Massachusetts Institute of Technology.

So we have a very esteemed group of witnesses today, and we appreciate you being with us. And, again, if you could summarize in 5 minutes, we will have a good dialogue on this.

Dr. Aron, you may proceed.

STATEMENT OF LEON ARON, PH.D., RESIDENT SCHOLAR AND DIRECTOR OF RUSSIAN STUDIES, THE AMERICAN ENTERPRISE INSTITUTE

Mr. ARON. Thank you very much, Mr. Chairman, Ranking Member, members of the committee.

On the morning of July 19, 2012, gunshots and car bombs explosion woke up Kazan, the capital of Tatarstan, Russia's largest autonomous republic and the home of its largest Muslim ethnicity, the Tatars. The shots hit Valiulla Yakupov, Deputy Mufti of Tatarstan, in charge of education in Islamic studies. The bomb went off under the car of the Chief Mufti of Tatarstan, Ildus Fayzov. Fayzov was badly injured. Yakupov was killed.

Appointed only a year before, both men were moderate clerics, determined to oppose what they saw as the encroachment of fundamentalism, Salafism in Tatarstan, and to strengthen the traditional moderate Hanafi madhab, which is one of the five major branches of Sunni Islam. Lest anyone miss the terrorists' point, a cavalcade of cars, under the black-and-white banners of global jihadists, raced through downtown Kazan shortly after the attack.

I think the July 19 attack, in retrospect, could be viewed as a watershed. Two decades after the first Chechen war, the Russian jihad may be reaching a tipping point at which the center of gravity of militant Islamic fundamentalism is shifting from North Caucasus to the more urban and densely populated European Russian heartland, the home of 13 million Muslims, especially Tatars and Bashkirs, Russia's second-largest Muslim group, that are very

4

close to Tatars both ethnically and geographically. If this trend continues, the consequences for the largest Muslim country in Europe, and Russia has an estimated Muslim population of 20 million, could be ominous.

Let me mention five underlying factors, all of which continue to operate today as risk factors that increase the likelihood of terrorist attacks in Russia and heighten Russia's vulnerability to such attack.

Number one, Russia has not been able to evade the pan-European phenomenon. That is the turn to radical Islam of a fraction of seemingly assimilated and integrated European Muslim population, especially its young people.

Two, the exposure after the fall of the Soviet Union of an estimated tens of thousands of Russian Muslims to Salafism and Wahhabism in the course of theological studies in the Middle East. In their return to Tatarstan and Bashkortostan, some of the newly minted imams have increasingly turned away from the traditional, moderate Hanafi madhab and toward Salafism and Wahhabism. According to Russian experts, imams that share Wahhabi views preach at dozens of the over 1,000 mosques in Tatarstan.

Three, Russia is now home to millions of guest workers, Muslims from Central Asia: An estimated 2 million Uzbeks, between 1 and 2 million Tajiks, and around 1 million Kyrgyz. There are an estimated 2½ million of only registered migrants from Central Asian Moscow alone, making the Russian capital the largest Muslim city in Europe.

Often without work permits, marginalized culturally and ethically, and often subjected to abuse, extortion, and not infrequently to racist violence, many of the men, understandably, turn to their faith and the faith of their grandparents as a means to sustain their dignity. Unfortunately, as reported in the Russian media, at least some fall under the influence of radical clerics and, more importantly and recently, recruiters from ISIS.

According to the reports in the Russian media, most, if not all ISIS fighters from Central Asia have been recruited at the construction sites in Russia, especially Moscow, including an estimated 400 ethnic Uzbeks fighting with ISIS in Syria. All of them were recruited outside of Uzbekistan, including their reported leader, Nusrat Nazarov.

Number four, given the permeability of borders, the recruitment, and the proselytizing effort that has been doubled and tripled by ISIS in Central Asia, especially Uzbekistan, Kyrgyzstan, and Tajikistan, given the flow of people, such efforts are likely to result in the increasing radicalization of the elements of the Central Asian diaspora in Russia. If you add to this the fact that, with Russia on the ground now in Syria, adding to other risks of Putin's decision is also the fact that the probability of retaliatory terrorist strikes inside Russia are increasing.

The final point, the Secretary of the Russian Security Council, Nikolai Patrushev, said that, at the moment, Russian authorities do not have the means to stem the flow of volunteers to ISIS. The Russian Foreign Ministry estimates that there are around 2,400 Russian speakers among the jihadists in Syria, while the total Russian nationals and those from the former Soviet Union in the ranks of ISIS could be as high as 5,000. Today, Russian is the third-most popular ISIS language after Arabic and English.

How long will it be before the veterans of ISIS, coming back to Russia, decide to join a fight for a Russian caliphate inside Russia?

Mr. Chairman, let me conclude on this. Like overwhelming majorities of Muslims everywhere, most Russian Muslims and the migrants from Central Asia practice their religion peacefully, abhor violence, and are good citizens and patriots of their countries. Yet, as we have learned only too well in the 14 years since 9/11, the radicalization of even a small minority, not registered by any public opinion polls, can inflict incalculable damage and cost thousands of lives.

If the evidence that I outlined today does not amount to a significant increase in national and international terrorism, I will be the first to acknowledge and celebrate my error. But having largely missed the rise of Chechen terrorism, al-Qaeda, and ISIS, we would be far better off wrong than sorry.

Thank you very much.

[The prepared statement of Mr. Aron follows:]

American Enterprise Institute for Public Policy Research

Testimony at the Hearing on "The Threat of Islamic Extremism in Russia"
The House Committee on Foreign Affairs
Subcommittee on Europe, Eurasia, and Emerging Threats

The Expansion of Russia's Radical Islamism Outside the North Caucasus

Leon Aron, Ph.D.

Resident Scholar and Director of Russian Studies

American Enterprise Institute

September 30, 2015

Thank you Mr. Chairman.

Mr. Chairman, Ranking Member, Members of the Committee:

On the morning of July 19, 2012, Kazan the capital of Tatarstan, Russia's largest autonomous republic and home of its largest Muslim ethnicity, the Tatars, was awakened by six gun shots and, fifteen minutes later, the explosion of a car bomb. The shots were aimed at Valiulla Yakupov, Deputy Mufti of Tatarstan and leading theologian who supervised Islamic education in Tatarstan, as he walked out of his apartment building. The bomb went off under the car of Yakupov's boss, Mufti Ildus Fayzov. Yakupov was killed instantly. Fayzov was badly injured.[1]

Since their appointment a year before, Fayzov and Yakupov had been crusading "anti-Wahhabists," out to strengthen the traditional, moderate Hanafi *madhab* (one of the five major branches of Sunni Islam) by firing imams and madrasa teachers who they felt were too tolerant of the more radical Salafism, including the Imam of the of Kazan's main *mechet* (mosque) Kul Sharif.[2] Lest anyone miss the terrorists' point, a cavalcade of cars driving under the black-and-white banners of global jihadists raced through downtown Kazan.[3]

Yet there was more to what happened that morning in Kazan than an internecine struggle within Europe's oldest and, until a decade or so ago, most assimilated Muslim minority. The July 19th attacks may well have been a watershed: two decades after the first Chechen war, the Russian Jihad may be reaching a tipping point at which the center of gravity of militant Islamic fundamentalism has begun to shift from the North Caucasus to the more urban and densely populated European Russian heartland, the home of 13 million Muslims, especially Tatars and Bashkirs. If this trend continues, the consequences for the largest Muslim country in Europe (with an estimated Muslim population of 20 million) and the world at large could be ominous.

Although the most dramatic, the 2012 attack was only an instance of a trend. Here are a few more examples:

- Of European countries, Russia and Britain had the largest number of their nationals at Guantanamo Bay prison: nine each. The Russian nationals included some of the longest held prisoners. Six out of nine were ethnic Tatars.[4]

- Awaiting sentencing after a trial last month in the federal district court in Richmond is a former commander of the Taliban-affiliated Haqqani Network in Afghanistan -- the first Taliban officer tried in a civilian court in the United States.[5] The defendant, Irek Hamidullin, is an ethnic Tatar from the most radicalized of Tatarstan's largest cities, Naberezhnye Chelny, which a leading

---

[1] http://kazanweek.ru/article/4276/
[2] ibid.

[3] http://www.regnum.ru/news/polit/1670767.html
[4] http://projects.nytimes.com/guantanamo/country/russia
http://www.jamestown.org/single/?tx_ttnews%5btt_news%5d=3258&no_cache=1#.Va1ElKRVhHx
[5] http://www.voanews.com/content/ap-unusual-terror-case-going-to-trial-in-us-court-in-virginia/2886773.html

Russian expert called "a focal point for Salafism in Tatarstan."[6]

- In November 2013 a rocket attack was mounted against a major Russian oil-refining facility in Nizhnekamsk, Tatarstan. The assailants used self-made Qassam missiles associated with the Palestinian Hamas.

- In May 2013, National Anti-Terrorist Committee (NAK) troops engaged in a firefight with a terrorist cell in the town of Orekhovo-Zuevo, 85 kilometers from Moscow, where the terrorists had travelled allegedly to engage in bombing attacks in the Russian capital. Two of them were killed and one wounded and captured. All three were ethnic Bashkirs, Russia's second largest Muslim ethnic group after the Tatars and very close to them ethnically and geographically.

- In the early 2000s, the so-called Uigur-Bulgar Jamaat (UBJ) was set up by Al Qaeda in the border areas between Afghanistan and Pakistan. Among its members were Tatars, Bashkirs and Uighurs from China and Kazakhstan.[7] Reportedly organized with the "direct participation" of Osama bin Laden,[8] the UBJ was ordered by Al Qaeda to "create a network of cells" throughout Russia.[9] Until the Russian authorities blocked the Jamaat's site in 2011, it posted Russian-language video and radio materials, including interviews with Russian "resistance fighters" inside the Jamaat.[10]

- Between 2006 and 2008 a UBJ cell was set up in Bashkortostan. Its leader, the 36-year old ethnic Russian convert Abdul Mudzhib (Pavel Dorokhov) was reported to have trained in Taliban and Al Qaeda camps in the mid-1990s and again in 2006-7.[11] Dorokhov was killed while resisting arrest by Russian special forces in August 2008. His deputy was sentenced to 15 years at a "strict regime" colony. According to the trial documents, they recruited members to "prepare terrorist acts against vital objects of Bashkortostan and against law enforcement personnel."[12] Two years later, eight members of the UBJ were arrested in Bashkortostan.[13]

- One of the UBJ leaders, an ethnic Tatar by the name of Rais Mingaleev who had proclaimed himself "Amir of the Tatar Mujahidin" and travelled repeatedly to the training camps on the Afghani-Pakistani border,[14] was the mastermind of the attack on Fayzov and Yakupov. After Mingaleev's death, the actual killer of Yakupov, Robert Valeev, became the new leader of the "Tatar Jamaat." A year later, members of the Jamaat [were reported to be among the "militants from Russia" fighting in Syria.[15]

---

[6] Sergey Markedonov, CSIS, January 2013, "The Rise of Radical and Nonofficial Islamic Groups in Russia's Volga Region," pg. 18., http://goo.gl/LIrNiJ.

[7] http://www.business-gazeta.ru/text/69270/

[8] http://www.centrasia.ru/newsA.php?st=1351234020

[9] http://www.kommersant.ru/Doc/1014330

[10] http://www.business-gazeta.ru/text/69270/

[11] http://www.kommersant.ru/Doc/1014330 and http://www.kommersant.ru/doc/1207571

[12] http://www.kommersant.ru/doc/1207571

[13] http://www.business-gazeta.ru/text/69270/

[14] http://www.centrasia.ru/newsA.php?st=1351234020

[15] http://www.jamestown.org/single/?tx_ttnews%5Btt_news%5D=41049&no_cache=1#.VdI3N-nZr8F

■ According to the leader of Tatar Muslim "Public Center" in Naberezhnye Chelny, 200 Tatar "radical Muslims" were fighting in Syria in summer 2013[16] -- as were, according to the Federal Security Service (FSB) 50 Bashkirs.[17] In addition, "several dozen" Bashkirs were said to have been trained in terrorist camps in the area around the Pakistan-Afghanistan border.[18]

**

This possible shift of the center of gravity of the Russian jihad from the North Caucasus to European Russia has been long in the making. Let me mention just a few causes. Most of them continue to operate today as risk factors that increase the likelihood of terrorist attacks in Russia and heighten Russia's vulnerability to such attacks:

To begin, after the fall of the Soviet Union, the pent-up demand for religion and religious education, which affected Russian Muslims (as it did members of all other religious denominations of Russia) was met with a dearth of native clergy. As a result, an estimated "tens of thousands"[19] of Russian Muslims (many of them, future Russian imams) received education in the Middle East, mostly in Egypt, Saudi Arabia, Syria and Tunisia. [20] In the process, many of the students have been exposed to Salafism and Wahhabism – not just in such notoriously Salafi-leaning centers as the University of Medina,[21] the Jeddah University, [22]or the King Abdul-Aziz University in Saudi Arabia.[23] On their return to Tatarstan and Bashkortostan, some of these imams have increasingly turned away from the traditional, moderate *Hanafi* madhab (or school of Islamic theology) and toward the more fundamentalist Salafism or even Wahhabism. According to Russian experts Imams who share Wahhabi views preach and serve in dozens of the over Tatar 1,000 mosques, especially in Naberezhnye Chelny.[24]

■ Russia is now home to millions of guest workers, most of them from Muslim Central Asia. There are an estimated two and a half million of only registered migrants in Moscow alone,[25] making it the largest Muslim city in Europe.[26] Often without work permits; marginalized, culturally and

---

[16] http://www.regnum.ru/news/polit/1670767.html

[17] http://www.km.ru/v-rossii/2013/06/07/federalnaya-sluzhba-bezopasnosti-rf-fsb/712634-fsb-zavershila-likvidatsiyu-bandg;

[18] http://www.km.ru/v-rossii/2013/06/07/federalnaya-sluzhba-bezopasnosti-rf-fsb/712634-fsb-zavershila-likvidatsiyu-bandg;

[19] Alikberov, op.cit.

[20] http://www.interfax-religion.ru/?act=radio&div=1811

[21] http://www.nytimes.com/2014/08/23/opinion/isis-atrocities-started-with-saudi-support-for-salafi-hate.html?_r=0

[22] http://nationalinterest.org/commentary/the-great-salafi-gamble-7720

[23] http://orfonline.org/cms/export/orfonline/modules/orfpapers/attachments/wilson1_1374144886603.pdf

[24] Malashenko, Aleksey, Carnegie Endowment, August 31, 2012, "No Repeat of Chechnya," http://goo.gl/Xt3j9X. See also [24] Rais Suleimanov, "Salafism in Tatarstan: On the verge of war," *Agenstvo Politicheskikh Novostey*, December 15, 2010, http://newsland.com/news/detail/id/607026/

[25] http://www.mskagency.ru/materials/1609913

[26] http://www.ibtimes.com/moscow-largest-muslim-city-europe-faithful-face-discrimination-public-authorities-2020858

ethnically; and often subject to abuse, extortion, and, not infrequently, to racist violence many of these men understandably turn to the faith of their grandparents as a means to sustain dignity. As a result, Tajiks, or Kyrgyz, or Uzbeks who would not have known the way to the nearest mosque in Dushanbe, Bishkek or Tashkent have become zealous Muslims in Moscow, with at least some falling under the influence of radical clerics. As a result, Moscow has become the base for so-called spotters and recruiters for ISIS from all over Russia and the Soviet Union and a key way station on the road to Syria. No one knows precisely how many spotters and recruiters are working in the city, but the estimates run all the way to several hundred. Most troubling is the recent statement by the Secretary of the Security Council, Nikolai Patrushev that at the moment, Russian authorities do not have the means to stem the flow of volunteers to ISIS.[27] The Russian Foreign Ministry estimates that there are around 2,400 Russian- speakers among the jihadist in Syria,[28] while the total of Russian nationals and those from the former Soviet Union in the ranks of ISIS could be as high as 5,000.[29] Today, Russian is the third most popular ISIS language after Arabic and English.[30]

■ ISIS's recruitment effort from the post-Soviet states is likely to grow. According to Egypt's Administration for Religious Regulations, as Arab states clamped down on ISIS efforts the group's leadership decided that it would be "quite easy to recruit supporters" in Central Asia, along with a few other vulnerable spots around the world, because Muslims there are "numerous, not acquainted with the extremist ideology of the group, and have been inclined to trust Arab proselytizers."[31] Given the permeability of borders and relatively unimpeded flows of people, such efforts are likely to result in the increasing radicalization of the elements of the Central Asia diaspora in Russia. This danger factor will increase multi-fold should the Taliban continue to undermine the central authority in Kabul and almost certainly attempts to destabilize Central Asia, starting with Tajikistan.

■ How long will it be before the "surplus" of ISIS recruits is directed toward terrorism inside Russia? How many of Islamic State's former Russian soldiers, upon their return home, will take up the causes of the "Caliphate" inside Russia? As early as 2012, the Rector of the Russian Islamic University in Kazan, Rafik Mukhametshin warned that "long before the [2012] assassination in Kazan, experts talked about how the [Tatar] fighters will return home and some of them will continue to be in touch with radical Islamic forces. And I don't exclude the possibility that, trained elsewhere, they may emerge in Tatarstan – or have emerged already."[32]

■ Finally, adding to other multiple risks of Putin's decision to intervene militarily in Syria, is a significantly increased probability of retaliatory terrorist attacks inside Russia.

Clearly, as the risk factors and trends I have outlined, continue to exist, expand and converge, the forecast for Russia and the world is far from optimistic.

---

[27] http://www.novayagazeta.ru/news/1694665.html
[28] "Putin Said to Plan Islamic State Strike With or Without U.S." Bloomberg, September 23, 2015
[29] http://lenta.ru/news/2015/06/17/igil/
[30] http://ria.ru/world/20150619/1079078702.html
[31] ria.ru/world/20150813/1181220263.html, in Paul Goble, "Window on Eurasia. August 14, 2015.
[32] http://www.business-gazeta.ru/text/69270/

In conclusion, let me make one point very clear. Like overwhelming majorities of Muslims everywhere, most Russian Muslims practice their religion peacefully, abhor violence, and are good citizens and patriots of their country. Yet as we have learned only too well in the 14 years since 9/11, the radicalization of a small minority, usually not registered by opinion polls and denied by the authorities and traditional clergy, can inflict incalculable damage and cost thousands of lives.

If the evidence outlined in this article does not result in a significant increase in national and international terrorism, I will be the first to acknowledge and celebrate my error. But having largely missed the rise of Chechen terrorism, Al Qaeda, and ISIS, we would be far better off wrong than sorry.

***

STATEMENT OF MR. SIMON SARADZHYAN, ASSISTANT DIREC-TOR, U.S.–RUSSIA INITIATIVE TO PREVENT NUCLEAR TER-RORISM, BELFER CENTER FOR SCIENCE AND INTER-NATIONAL AFFAIRS, HARVARD UNIVERSITY

Mr. SARADZHYAN. Mr. Chairman and distinguished members of the committee, thank you for inviting me to participate in what I believe is a very important event.

I will present my view on prospects for U.S.-Russian cooperation in countering terrorism, and I will start with an observation made by Winston Churchill, who is often quoted saying that Russia is a riddle wrapped in a mystery inside an enigma. Fewer, though, remember the remainder of that saying, which is that perhaps there is a key, and that key is Russia's national interest when it comes to discerning Russian actions.

There is no strategic document, Russian strategic document or statement that would offer a hierarchy of vital national interests, but I have taken liberty to distill some of the statements to build such a hierarchy in the statement that you have. Of these interests, at least three of seven vital national interests to Russia, at least three are affected by the political violence in the Middle East. And of these three interests, which are prevent insurgencies in Russia, in areas adjacent to Russia; prevent large-scale terrorist attacks on Russia and its allies; and prevent the proliferation of weapons of mass destruction, particularly nuclear weapons, to countries and also nonstate actors, at least two of those interests converge with U.S. vital national interests as formulated by the Commission on America's National Interests in 2000 and subsequent projects.

So, therefore, both countries share an interest in ensuring that the dual threat that emanates from the Middle East insurgency there is contained, and that comes to countering the rise of ISIS, continuing to dismantle or keep al-Qaeda on the run, as well as denying these and other terrorist organizations any access to weapons of mass destruction, and particularly to nuclear weapons.

I should note that, even though there are 30,000 recruits, reportedly, from foreign countries in ISIL and at least 4,500 of them are estimated to have come from the West, Russia and its allies are more exposed to the threat posed by ISIS, if only because of the proximity. And, as Dr. Aron has pointed out, there are various estimates.

The latest estimates have come from the Federal Security Service, and it is that 2,400 Russian nationals are in ISIS, and about 3,000 nationals of Central Asian republics are also in ISIS. That is a potent force.

We shouldn't also discount al-Qaeda's al-Nusrah Front, which has its own unit that consists of natives of Russia's North Caucasus, but also the republics of Central Asia, and that unit counts about 1,500.

So imagine what would happen if all these individuals come home, whether because ISIL prevails or whether because ISIL is defeated, but these individuals are not apprehended or eliminated.

I should note that both organizations, ISIL and al-Qaeda, have maintained ties with the insurgents and terrorist networks in the North Caucasus. This summer saw ISIS establish a vilayat, a sort of province in the North Caucasus; and the Emirate Caucasus, the umbrella terrorist organization, operates in the North Caucasus, has had longstanding ties with al-Qaeda, and its leaders have praised Ayman al-Zawahiri as their leader.

So no surprise that Russian officials, including Foreign Minister Lavrov and Secretary of the Security Council Patrushev, have described ISIS as the main threat to Russia and the main threat to global security, respectively. On the U.S. side, there is less agreement on whether ISIS represents a top threat, but I think the FBI Director has been quoted as saying that it is a top threat to U.S. national security.

So since neither the United States nor Russia can tolerate the further existence of a quasi-state in the form of ISIS in the Middle East, and both countries need to counter al-Qaeda and keep it on the run and reduce its possibilities, I would argue there is definitely ground for potential cooperation.

Now, that is impeded by different approaches toward Syria, although I believe—and Russian officials have said officially—that Russia is not married to Assad. So I think in the longer term there is an opportunity for a transition to a coalition government that would represent Assad's key constituencies—Alawites, Kurds, and also moderate sections of the Syrian opposition.

For now, the U.S.-Russian cooperation can be, though, limited to fighting ISIL in Iraq, and that could include joint operations, which is something U.S. and Russian special forces have done on a very low scale in Afghanistan. It could include providing more arms and more training to the Iraqi Armed Forces and the Kurds fighting ISIL, and it could, of course, include disrupting financing, which is not a counterterrorism tactic per se, but is an important element of countering such organizations.

But even looking beyond that, countering terrorism with force alone would not suffice. So there are certain root causes and contributing factors that I am not going to list, but are in the statement, that both Russia and the United States need to address as they think how to defeat terrorists not only in the Middle East, or containment, but also in their own countries.

Of the deep-rooted and structural causes, I would point out relative socioeconomic deprivation, historical grievances, poor quality of governance, and political instability are factors that facilitate this violence. I would point out the spread of violent ideologies and, primarily, the militant form of Salafia, or so-called ''Wahhabism,'' as Dagestani officials call it.

And finally, the third group of causes, motivational causes I would point out are the abuses of the population. If there is anything that creates grievances, it is the abuses of the population at the hands of authorities.

So let me conclude by saying that cooperation between the United States and Russia against terrorism in general, and ISIS and al-Qaeda in particular, will not only significantly advance international efforts to contain these organizations' expansion within and without Iraq and adjacent countries, but it can also help to stop the slide toward a new Cold War between the West and Russia in the wake of the Ukraine crisis, although these factors are not exactly—there is no avoiding it. I mean, the Ukrainian crisis will have to be resolved regardless, but that cooperation—let me repeat—will help to stop the slide toward a new Cold War.

Thank you.

[The prepared statement of Mr. Saradzhyan follows:]

Simon Saradzhyan
Research Fellow and Assistant Director of U.S.-Russia Initiative to Prevent Nuclear Terrorism
Belfer Center for Science and International Affairs, Harvard Kennedy School
U.S. House of Representatives Committee on Foreign Affairs
September 30, 2015
The Threat of Islamist Extremism in Russia

U.S. and Russia Share a Vital Interest in Countering Terrorism
By Simon Saradzhyan

Can the United States and Russia cooperate against the threat posed by the Islamic State of Iraq and Syria and other international terrorist organizations, even though the bilateral relationship has deteriorated in the wake of the crisis in Ukraine? My answer is they can and they will if they act in their best interest.

When trying to underscore the difficulty of predicting the Kremlin's next steps, many Russia watchers in the West in general and in the U.S. in particular habitually cite Winston Churchill's famous description of Russia as "riddle wrapped in a mystery inside an enigma." Few however, recall the remainder of that 1939 adage by one of Great Britain's greatest statesmen: "But perhaps there is a key. That key is Russian national interest."

When explaining what drives their policies, Russian president Vladimir Putin and his advisors routinely make general references about the need to protect or advance Russia's national interests. Occasionally they also reveal what interests they think Russia shares with other countries. For instance, in an April 2015 interview, Vladimir Putin said Russia shares key interests with the United States and that the countries need to work together. Putin mentioned countering proliferation of weapons of mass destruction, fighting international organized crime and terrorism, eradicating poverty in the world, making global economy "more democratic and balanced," as well as "making global order more democratic" among these common interests.

But while weighing common interests with specific countries, neither Russian authorities nor the country's think-tanks have offered a comprehensive of list what constitutes Russia's national interests or what their order of importance is. I have taken the liberty of constructing a hierarchy of Russia's vital national interests, distilling from Russian leaders' statements and national strategies. I then squared that hierarchy against the list of U.S. vital national interests -- as formulated in two U.S. reports on the subject[1]-- to identify areas of convergence and divergence. The result of my effort is represented in the table below.

Russia's vital national interests (in order of importance):	U.S. vital national interests:	Converge (C)/ Diverge(D)/ No equivalent (NE):
Prevent, deter and reduce threats of secession from Russia; insurgency within Russia or in areas adjacent to Russia; and armed conflicts	Not available;	No equivalent;

[1] Ellsworth, Robert, Andrew Goodpaster, and Rita Hauser. Co-Chairs. *America's National Interests: A Report from The Commission on America's National Interests, 2000.* Washington, D.C.: Report for Commission on America's National Interests, July 2000; Allison, Graham, Robert D. Blackwill, Dimitri K. Simes, and Paul J. Saunders. *Russia and U.S. National Interests: Why Should Americans Care?.* Washington, D.C. and Cambridge, Mass: Report for Center for the National Interest and Belfer Center for Science and International Affairs, Harvard Kennedy School, October 2011;

waged against Russia, its allies or in vicinity of Russian frontiers;		
Prevent emergence of hostile individual or collective regional hegemonies or failed states on Russian borders, ensure Russia is surrounded by friendly states among which Russia can play a lead role and cooperation with which it can thrive;	Maintain a balance of power in Europe and Asia that promotes peace and stability with a continuing U.S. leadership role;	Russian and U.S. interests more diverge than converge;
Establish and maintain productive relations, upon which Russian national interests hinge to a significant extent, with core European Union members, the United States and China;	Establish and maintain productive relations, consistent with American national interests, with nations that could become strategic adversaries, China and Russia;	Converge (partially);
Ensure the viability and stability of major markets for major flows of Russian exports and imports;	Ensure the viability and stability of major global systems (trade, financial markets, supplies of energy, and the environment);	Converge;
Ensure steady development and diversification of the Russian economy and its integration into global markets;	Not available;	No equivalent;
Prevent neighboring nations from acquiring nuclear arms and their long-range delivery systems on Russian borders; secure nuclear weapons and materials;	Prevent the use and slow the spread of nuclear weapons and other weapons of mass destruction, secure nuclear weapons and materials, and prevent proliferation of intermediate and long-range delivery systems for nuclear weapons;	Converge, but differ in methods of advancing this interest;
Prevent large-scale or sustained terrorist attacks on Russia;	Prevent large-scale or sustained terrorist attacks on the American Homeland;	Converge;
Ensure Russian allies' survival and their active cooperation with Russia;	Ensure U.S. allies' survival and their active cooperation with the U.S. in shaping an international system in which U.S. can thrive;	No equivalent;
Not available;	Prevent the emergence of	No equivalent.

	hostile major powers or failed states on US borders;	

As clear from the list above, Russian vital interests partially diverge with those of the U.S. only in the post-Soviet neighborhood, while either converging in other areas or having no equivalent on the U.S. side. The two countries' interests now clearly converge when it comes to preventing the use and slowing the spread of nuclear weapons and other weapons of mass destruction and to reducing the threat of large-scale terrorist attacks on themselves and their allies.

Both of these threats have been emanating from the instability and violence in the Middle East, where such terrorist organizations as the Islamic State of Iraq and Syria (ISIS) and al-Qaeda operate with the former controlling parts of Syria and Iraq. Both ISIS and al-Qaeda have displayed strong interest in acquiring weapons of mass destruction and ISIS has also allegedly used crude chemical weapons. If either of these organizations were to acquire nuclear weapons[2], neither would hesitate to use them against Russia and the U.S. and their allies if such use would advance them toward their goal of building a caliphate. Both of these organizations have also recruited citizens of America, European Union countries and Russia to fight in their ranks as well as encouraged them to conduct attacks at home.

Russia and its allies are more exposed to the terrorist threat emanating from the Middle East, particularly as ISIS contemplates expanding the territory it controls as it pursues the goal of building a caliphate. Russia's First Deputy Director of Federal Security Sergei Smirnov estimated in September 2015 that there about 2,400 Russian nationals fighting on the side of the Islamic State. IS' commander in Syria is Tarkhan Batirashvili, an ethnic Chechen who hails from the Republic of Georgia's Pankisi Gorge and who goes by the nom de guerre Abu Omar al-Shishani. There are also 3,000 nationals of Central Asian republics, of which three are members of the Russian-led Collective Security Allies, fighting in ISIS ranks, according to Smirnov.[3]

In addition to IS, nationals of Russia and other former Soviet republics are also fighting in structures affiliated with al-Qaeda in Levant. One of such structures, Jaish al-Muhajireen wal-Ansar, reportedly employs 1,500 Chechen, Uzbek and Tajik fighters and pledged allegiance to al Qaeda's Syria wing Nusra Front in September 2015, according to the Syrian Observatory for Human Rights.[4] This unit, led by ethnic Chechen Salahuddin al Shishani, is formally a part of the so-called Emirate Caucasus terrorist organization, which is based in Russia's North Caucasus. It should be noted that Salahuddin al Shishani's real name was originally Giorgi Kushtanashvili, but he then changed into Feizullah Margoshvili, which indicates that he also hails from Georgia's Pankisi Gorge.[5]

---

[2] See the following two publications for summary of al-Qaeda and ISIS' interest in nuclear weapons: Bunn, Matthew, and Yuri Morozov, Rolf Mowatt-Larrsen, Simon Saradzhyan, William Tobey, Viktor I. Yesin, and Pavel S. Zolotarev. The U.S.-Russia Joint Threat Assessment of Nuclear Terrorism. Cambridge, Mass., : Report for Belfer Center for Science and International Affairs, Harvard Kennedy School, Institute for U.S. and Canadian Studies, June 6, 2011; and Simon Saradzhyan. *The U.S.-Russia Initiative to Prevent Nuclear Terrorism Newsletter: May June 2015.* Harvard University, July 14, 2015.

[3] "Moscow says about 2,400 Russians fighting with Islamic State: RIA," *Reuters,* September 18, 2015.

[4] "Insurgent group pledges allegiance to al Qaeda's Syria wing," Reuters, September 23, 2015.

[5] Joanna Paraszczuk, "Who is Salahuddin al Shishani?" From Chechnya to Syria, April 2015.

As it is known, Al-Qaeda's leader Ayman al-Zawahiri declared war on ISIS in September 2015. The rivalry between these two organizations has trickled down to Russia's North Caucasus, where the leadership of Emirate Caucasus has essentially sided with al-Qaeda only to see a group of local field commanders branch out to establish an Islamic State *vilayat* in the North Caucasus in June 2015. But while fighting for supremacy, both leaders of ISIS and al-Qaeda and their supporters in the North Caucasus are firmly aligned with the vision of caliphate, which they hope to build in the Middle East and expand to the North Caucasus and other regions of Russia with significant Muslim populations.

Now imagine what would happen if ISIS succeeds in maintaining a quasi-state in parts of Syria and Iraq, and these nationals try to repeat this success at their homes as ISIS will seek to expand the 'caliphate' to post-Soviet space. Given these risks, it should come as no surprise that Russia's Foreign Minister Sergei Lavrov and Security Council secretary Nikolai Patrushev describe ISIS as Russia's main enemy and main threat to global security respectively. Washington is also concerned about ISIS' rise. The FBI's director James Comey has recently been quoted as saying that ISIS poses the greatest danger to U.S. homeland, though there is no consensus in the U.S. leadership on whether and what terrorist organization represents the top threat to U.S. national security. According to Comey, ISIS has developed a "chaotic spider web" in the United States. "Those people exist in every state," Comey said in February 2015. Some of these individuals have allegedly planned terrorist attacks in the continental U.S. homeland, including plans to blow up Coney Island and kill U.S. law-enforcers and soldiers. [6] According to Representative Michael McCaul, chairman of the U.S. House of Representatives' homeland security committee, the U.S. foiled over 60 terrorist attacks by "ISIS followers" in 2014 alone.[7] ISIS has also been reported to plan attacks in Europe and some of its followers, such as Amedy Coulibaly, have unfortunately succeeded in their plans. Overall, however, in spite of all the threats, ISIS appears to have refrained from attempting to launch large-scale terrorist campaigns in either U.S., EU or Russia.

It should be noted that governments of U.S. and Russia have not always seen eye-to-eye on what counter-terrorism cooperation of the two countries should entail. As Thomas Graham and I note in a recent article, the United States was interested in intelligence sharing on Al Qaeda in the 2000s; while Russia at that time wanted information on exiled Chechens that they suspected of supporting violent separatism.[8] But the rise of the Islamic State should begin to close the gap in the U.S. and Russian governments' perception of the nature of the terrorist threat emanating from parts of the Middle East. For perhaps the first time in the counterterrorist struggle, the United States and Russia share a common concrete enemy in the form of ISIS.[9] Neither the U.S. nor Russia can afford to tolerate the existence of a terrorist quasi-state, which is actively training nationals of their countries and interested in acquiring weapons of mass destruction. Nor can leaders of the U.S., Russia, and their allies sit and wait for ISIS to decide if it should escalate from executing citizens of Western and post-Soviet states to launching large-scale terrorist campaigns against them. Many common Russians would support Russia's participation in

---

[6] "ISIS present in all 50 states, FBI director say," ABC7 Chicago, February 25, 2015.
[7] "U.S. missed Chattanooga attack but foiled 'over 60' Isis-linked plots: security chair," the Guardian, July 19, 2015.
[8] Graham, Thomas and Simon Saradzhyan. "ISIS' Worst Nightmare: The U.S. and Russia Teaming Up on Terrorism." *The National Interest*, Tuesday, February 10, 2015.
[9] Graham, Thomas and Simon Saradzhyan. "ISIS' Worst Nightmare: The U.S. and Russia Teaming Up on Terrorism." *The National Interest*, Tuesday, February 10, 2015.

international efforts to rout ISIS. The share of Russians who think Russia should fight ISIS is more than twice as large (36%) as the share of those who hold the opposite view (15%). Moreover, two-thirds of those who believe Russia should fight ISIS also think their countries should do so in cooperation with Western countries, according to a recent poll by Russia's Public Opinion Foundation.

The governments of Russia, the United States, and their allies could utilize the positive momentum, which their cooperation in securing an agreement between P5+1 and Iran has created, to coordinate their actions against ISIS. While such coordination in Syria is impeded by disagreements over whether and how Bashir al-Assad should depart from power, there is an opportunity for Washington and Moscow to cooperate against ISIS in Iraq. The United States and Russia could begin to cooperate against ISIS by taking small, concrete, pragmatic steps, mirroring their cooperation in the initial phases of the U.S.-led campaign in Afghanistan. These steps could include sharing intelligence on ISIS and cooperating in joint special operations against key targets. The two countries have acquired limited, but valuable experience in such joint operations in Afghanistan where officers of Russia's Federal Drug Police reportedly participated in ISAF raids on drug laboratories. Russia could also supply advisors, training programs and more arms to the Iraqi forces and Kurdish forces, in coordination with the West. Unfreezing military-to-military contacts between the U.S. and its NATO allies, and Russia, and reviving work of such elements of the bilateral U.S.-Russian presidential commission, as working groups on counter-terrorism, defense relations, military cooperation, and nuclear security, would facilitate such cooperation.

Of course, use of force is just one component of a successful comprehensive approach toward countering such strategies of political violence, as terrorism and insurgency. Both countries suffering from political violence and international coalitions built to assist them would also need to address factors behind such violence, which scholars of this phenomenon[10] classify as:

1. Deep-rooted or structural causes, which affect people's lives at a "rather abstract level," and which include relative socio-economic deprivation; historical grievances; poor quality of governance; and political instability.
2. Facilitator (or accelerator) causes which facilitate political violence, making it more attractive without being prime movers, and which include spread of violent ideologies; support; availability of capable leaders; youth bulge; scientific-technological progress; traditions of violence; difficulty of disengagement from violence; complex terrain.
3. Motivational causes that could be also defined as grievances that people actually experience, motivating them to act, including abuses at hands of authorities

Cooperation between U.S. and Russia against terrorism in general and ISIS and al-Qaeda in particular can not only significantly advance international efforts to first contain ISIS's expansion within and without Iraq and defeat this terrorist organization. Such cooperation can also help to stop the slide towards a new Cold War between the West and Russia in the wake of the Ukraine crisis.

---

[10] For classification of causes behind political violence, see, for example, Sagramoso, Domitilla. "Violence and conflict in the Russian North Caucasus." *International Affairs* 83, no. 4 (2007): 681-705, and Bjorgo, Tore. "Introduction", in Bjorgo, Tore, ed. *Root Causes of Terrorism: Myths, reality and ways forward*. Routledge, 2004, 3-4.

STATEMENT OF MARK N. KATZ, PH.D., PROFESSOR OF GOVERNMENT AND POLITICS, SCHOOL OF POLICY, GOVERNMENT, AND INTERNATIONAL AFFAIRS, GEORGE MASON UNIVERSITY

Mr. KATZ. Mr. Chairman, distinguished members, thank you so much for the invitation to speak to you today. I would like to address the Syrian aspect of this issue.

Unlike in Ukraine, where Moscow has openly declared that its motive for intervention and support for separatist forces is being undertaken to counter the West, Russian officials have characterized their support for the Assad regime in Syria as actually being in Western interests—even if Western governments do not quite seem to understand this—since it serves the common goal of combating the Islamic State.

Russian President Vladimir Putin recently described the Assad regime as an important ally in the fight against the Islamic State. "It is evident," he stated recently, "that without an active participation of the Syrian authorities and military, without participation of the Syrian army inside the territory, as the military say, in the fight against Islamic State, terrorists cannot be expelled from that country and from the region on the whole."

Russian Foreign Minister Sergey Lavrov described the Assad regime as a crucial ally against Islamic State. He declared that, "The Syrian President is the commander in chief of probably the most capable ground force fighting terrorism. To give up such an opportunity, ignore the capabilities of the Syrian army as a partner and ally in the fight against the Islamic State, means to sacrifice the entire region's security to some geopolitical moods and calculations."

Now, while the West may not like Assad, Russian officials and commentators are saying his authoritarian regime is preferable to an even worse one that Islamic State would establish that would pose a real threat to Western, as well as Russian interests. Furthermore, Assad regime forces are needed in order to stop Islamic State from taking over more or even the rest of Syria. Western insistence that Assad must step down, then, is foolish since this would gravely weaken the forces fighting against Islamic State. The West, then, should work with Moscow and the Assad regime against the common threat and not against them.

This argument is based on the premise that the Assad regime is actively fighting against Islamic State. There have been numerous reports, though, that the Assad regime and the Islamic State have actually not been fighting with each other or not doing so very much. A widely quoted study by IHS Jane's Terrorism and Insurgency Center at the end of last year noted that the Assad regime's "counterterrorism operations . . . skew heavily toward groups whose names aren't ISIS. Of 982 counterterrorism operations for the year, up through November 21, 2014, just 6 percent directly targeted ISIS."

In February of this year, TIME magazine reported on a Sunni businessman with close ties to the Assad regime describing various forms of actual cooperation between the Assad regime and the Islamic State, including how the Assad regime buys oil from Islamic State-controlled oil facilities, how Syria's two main mobile phone operators provide service and send repair teams to IS-controlled areas, and how Damascus allows food shipment to the IS capital, Raqqa.

At the beginning of June 2015, U.S. Embassy Damascus accused the Syrian Government of providing air support to an advance by Islamic State militants against other opposition groups north of Aleppo.

In July, Turkish intelligence sources claimed that ''an agreement was made between the Assad regime and Islamic State to destroy the Free Syrian Army in the country's north.''

Now, why would the Assad regime not fight against the Islamic State and even cooperate with it? Both of them have an interest in weakening their common foes—other Syrian opposition groups being supported by Turkey, Saudi Arabia, Qatar, and others.

Moscow and Damascus, of course, vehemently deny that the Assad regime and the Islamic State are not fighting each other and are even cooperating against their common foes. The numerous reports that this is what is happening, as well as the compelling nature of the ''enemy of my enemy is my friend'' logic at work here, though, point to their credibility. And if these reports are true, then certain implications follow.

If Assad and the Islamic State are not really fighting each other, but the Assad regime is losing ground, then its weakening is due primarily to the non-Islamic State forces backed by Turkey and the Gulf Arabs.

Russian military support to the Assad regime is likely to be used primarily against those forces that are most threatening to Damascus—i.e., the Free Syrian Army, the al-Nusrah Front, and all of the others—and not against the Islamic State, which is less threatening to it.

Russian calls for the West to work with Moscow and Damascus in the fight against the Islamic State, then, are really intended to elicit Western acquiescence to increased Russian support for Assad regime efforts to combat its more threatening non-Islamic State opponents as well as to divide Western governments that fear the Islamic State more than the Assad regime, on the one hand, from Turkey and the Gulf Arab states, which are more focused on supporting the downfall of the Assad regime through supporting its non-Islamic State opponents on the other.

What all this suggests is that the recent increase in Russian military involvement in Syria is motivated much less by a desire to combat the Islamic State than by the desire to protect the Assad regime against its more active non-Islamic State opponents as well as to blunt the actions of Western and Middle Eastern actors aimed at supporting them.

Thank you.

[The prepared statement of Mr. Katz follows:]

House Committee on Foreign Affairs
Subcommittee on Europe, Eurasia, and Emerging Threats

"The Threat of Islamist Extremism in Russia"

September 30, 2015

Mark N. Katz, Ph.D.
Professor of Government and Politics
School of Policy, Government, and International Affairs
George Mason University

Who Is Putin Really Protecting Assad From?

Unlike in Ukraine where Moscow has openly declared that its motive for intervention and support for separatist forces as being undertaken to counter the West, Russian officials have characterized their support for the Assad regime in Syria as actually being in Western interests—even if Western governments do not quite seem to understand this—since it serves the common goal of combatting the Islamic State (also known as IS, ISIS and ISIL).

Russian President Vladimir Putin recently described the Assad regime as an important ally in the fight against IS. "It is evident," he stated recently, "that without an active participation of the Syrian authorities and military, without participation of the Syrian army inside the territory, as the military say, in [the] fight against Islamic State, terrorists cannot be expelled from that country and from the region on the whole." http://tass.ru/en/politics/821110

Russian Foreign Minister Sergei Lavrov described the Assad regime as a crucial ally against IS. He declared that, "the Syrian president is the commander-in-chief of probably the most capable ground force fighting terrorism, to give up such an opportunity, ignore the capabilities of the Syrian army as a partner and ally in the fight against the Islamic State means to sacrifice the entire region's security to some geopolitical moods and calculations." http://tass.ru/en/politics/821910

While the West may not like Assad, Russian officials and commentators are saying, his authoritarian regime is preferable to an even worse one that IS would establish that would pose a real threat to Western, as well as Russian, interests. Furthermore, Assad regime forces are needed in order to stop IS from taking over more—or even the rest—of Syria. Western insistence that Assad must step down, then, is foolish since this would gravely weaken the forces fighting against IS. The West, then, should work with Moscow and the Assad regime against the common IS threat, and not against them.

This argument is based on the premise that the Assad regime is actively fighting against IS. There have been numerous reports, though, that the Assad regime and IS have actually not been fighting with each other, or not doing so very much. A widely quoted study by IHS Jane's Terrorism and Insurgency Center at the end of last year noted that the Assad regime's "counterterrorism operations…skew heavily towards groups whose names aren't ISIS. Of 982 counterterrorism operations for the year up through Nov. 21 [2014], just 6 percent directly targeted ISIS." http://www.nbcnews.com/storyline/isis-uncovered/syria-isis-have-been-ignoring-each-other-battlefield-data-suggests-n264551

In February of this year, *TIME* reported on a Sunni businessman with close ties to the Assad regime describing various forms of actual cooperation between the Assad regime and IS, including how the Assad regime buys oil from IS-controlled oil facilities, how Syria's two main mobile phone operators provide service and send repair teams to IS-controlled areas, and how Damascus allows food shipments to the IS capital, Raqqa. http://time.com/3719129/assad-isis-asset/

At the beginning of June 2015, US Embassy Damascus "accused the Syrian government of providing air support to an advance by Islamic State militants against opposition groups north of Aleppo." http://www.theguardian.com/world/2015/jun/02/syria-isis-advance-on-aleppo-aided-by-assad-regime-air-strikes-us-says

In July, Turkish intelligence sources claimed that "an agreement was made between the Assad regime and ISIS to destroy the Free Syrian Army in the country's north." http://www.dailysabah.com/mideast/2015/07/02/isis-and-assad-cooperate-locally-on-mutual-interests-to-destroy-fsa

Why would the Assad regime not fight against IS and even cooperate with it? Both of them have an interest in weakening their common foes: other Syrian opposition groups being supported by Turkey, Saudi Arabia, Qatar, and other countries.

Moscow and Damascus, of course, vehemently deny that the Assad regime and IS are not fighting each other and are even cooperating against their common foes. The numerous reports that this is what is happening, as well as the compelling nature of the "enemy of my enemy is my friend" logic at work here, point to their credibility.

And if these reports are true, then certain implications follow:

--If Assad and IS are not really fighting each other, but the Assad regime is losing ground, then its weakening is due primarily to the non-IS forces backed by Turkey and the Gulf Arabs.

--Russian military support to the Assad regime is likely to be used primarily against those forces that are most threatening to Damascus (i.e., the Free Syrian Army, the Al Nusra Front, etc.), and not against IS which is less threatening to it.

--Russian calls for the West to work with Moscow and Damascus in the fight against IS, then, are really intended to elicit Western acquiescence to increased Russian support for Assad regime efforts to combat its more threatening non-IS opponents, as well as to divide Western governments that fear IS more than the Assad regime on the one hand from Turkey and Gulf Arab states which are more focused on supporting the downfall of the Assad regime through supporting its non-IS opponents on the other.

What all this suggests is that the recent increase in Russian military involvement in Syria is motivated much less by a desire to combat IS than by the desire to protect the Assad regime against its more active non-IS opponents as well as to blunt the actions of Western and Middle Eastern actors aimed at supporting them.

Mr. ROHRABACHER. Well, thank you all for this actually quite diverse view of what is going on and what we should do. I hope maybe by the end of this hearing we can actually come to some conclusions, but you are all so much wiser than I am, I assure you.

All right, Dr. Aron, Dr. Katz just basically called into question whether Assad is actually as anti-ISIL as we have been led to believe. Could you give us your assessment of that, please?

Mr. ARON. Well, I am sure Mark looked deep into that. I was concentrating largely on the spread of fundamentalism—militancy—inside Russia from the North Caucasus. But intuitively, you know, gangsters usually find common language—Stalin did with Hitler, for example—so I would not be surprised if that is the case. And in any case, they do come to blows, but first they take care of the pro-Western liberals. And, again, you know, that may not just apply directly to the Free Syrian Army, but, historically, I would think that that is probably quite accurate.

As somebody who has been dealing—you know, studying Putin and his ideology and his goals, I agree that, you know, even regardless of what Putin's plans are with respect to Assad, per se, I think they are secondary. I think the most important thing to Putin in Syria is what I call the implementation of the Putin doctrine, as I articulated a few years back, which is the recovery of geopolitical assets lost by the Soviet Union in the fall of the Soviet state. He wants to establish the presence of Russia in the Middle East as probably the dominant outside player. That is the first thing.

The second thing, let's not forget that, Assad or no Assad, the only thing, as a Russian analyst, top Russian pollster told me a couple years ago, the only thing that is going for this regime—I am talking about the Putin regime—is Putin's personal popularity, if you look at the public opinion polls. How does he get this popularity? He gets this popularity by embodying the thirst and the hunger for reestablishing Russia as a great power. This is what happened with Crimea, this is what happened with Ukraine, and now this is what is happening in Syria. I think this is the key motivational force, the key motivation for Putin to be present in Syria.

And one last thing, again, which has nothing to do with his support for Assad. There is a very serious concern, and both of the speakers touched on this, there is a very serious concern for what—you mentioned Churchill before, let me apply Churchill's definition of the Balkans—for the soft underbelly of Russia, which is the Central Asia. It consists of very unstable regimes, and the ISIS penetration and the Taliban subversion of those states brings ISIS and brings the Taliban to Russia's borders. This is another issue for, I think, motivated Putin.

Mr. ROHRABACHER. We have how many minutes before we vote? About 7 minutes.

I am going to yield several minutes to you now, and we will come back immediately after the two votes.

Mr. SIRES. I will wait until we get back.

Mr. ROHRABACHER. All right. We are in recess until immediately after the second vote.

[Recess.]

Mr. ROHRABACHER. The hearing is called to order. I will finish my questions after Mr. Sires has his chance.

Mr. SIRES. After you.

Mr. ROHRABACHER. Okay.

Look, again, there is a wonderful diversity of opinion here and a whole new concept, which I had not heard, and let me just ask then, from your testimony, you are suggesting that Assad is not someone who is as antiradical as we have been led to believe and that he would, and with Mr. Putin's involvement with Assad, is not going to direct them toward ISIL but direct them toward his own—or the nonaligned movement?

Mr. KATZ. I think that Assad, obviously, he is opposed to the jihadists, and they are opposed to him. I just think that the way in which they look at the question is one of, you know, a highly Machiavellian manner, and that is that, who is threatening Assad most now? It is not ISIS so much. It is these other opponents. And who threatens ISIS in many respects? In other words, it is a competition among the other Syrian opposition movements, so that they have a common interest at present that both would like to see the other opposition movements weakened. Now, that doesn't mean that they are going to be friends later on—in other words, they are preparing for the day that they will probably turn on each other—but at the moment, it seems that they are not so interested in fighting each other, that they both prefer to weaken the——

Mr. ROHRABACHER. So those two groups are not interested in fighting each other, and at least one of them is interested in fighting Assad, and Assad will then focus on, if we help him, only on that group and ISIL? So you are saying the ISIL forces are not at this point attacking Assad's military bases and things such as that and it is the group that we—by the way, just to note, I voted against arming that third force. I thought that was going to turn out the way things did in Iraq.

And so you are suggesting that that group now is, indeed, leading the fight against Assad and that ISIL is not?

Mr. KATZ. Well, obviously, it is many, many groups, in other words. It is not even as complicated as a three-cornered conflict. In other words, there are loads of actors involved here. But what it does seem is that at the moment, it is the opposition groups that are not ISIS that are most threatening to Assad; therefore, it is not surprising that Assad is concentrating his efforts on these particular forces.

Mr. ROHRABACHER. But we have seen reports that—and one of the reasons why we voted against doing this is that there have been defections by that third force, supposedly, to ISIL. In fact, one of the major leaders of that group defected, and the report that I read is he now commands a force half of which is made up of people from Chechnya.

Mr. KATZ. My memory of the report is that the moderates whom we supported defected to the al-Nusrah Front, which, of course, is hardly better, but it is not ISIS, that is for sure. But we are not a major actor in terms of, I think, external actors supporting the Syrian opposition. Obviously, it is the Saudis, the Turks, the Qataris, and others. And I think that they have their own agenda. I am not sure if it was ever possible to create this moderate third force. I don't think it necessarily was.

Mr. ROHRABACHER. Could you tell me what group, was it the third group that you are thinking about or was it ISIL that just captured the—I have trouble pronouncing it—I–D–L–I–B, the Idlib airbase, which was—I think it was 2 weeks ago? It was a major— it was a huge victory for—I assumed it was ISIL at the time, but it was a major defeat for Assad's forces.

Mr. KATZ. I am not positive which one it was actually who captured it. I just remember the very——

Mr. ROHRABACHER. So if it was ISIL and not this third force, the basis of your—that would go totally contrary to the basic which you are testifying today?

Mr. KATZ. I would just like to refer to the U.S. Embassy Damascus statement from earlier in June indicating that the U.S. accused the Syrian Government of providing air support to an advance by Islamic State militants against opposition groups north of Aleppo.

In other words, that there seems to be sort of a—not an actual alliance, but sort of an alliance of convenience, in many respects, between Assad and ISIS. If he has to give anything up, he would rather see it go to ISIS at present than his other opponents in order to bolster the argument that——

Mr. ROHRABACHER. But if that airbase, which was one of the major battles in the last 6 months, because they have been defending this with their lives and this was a major part of their strategy, if indeed that was an ISIL attack, that does basically contradict your theory.

Mr. KATZ. If it was an ISIL attack.

Mr. ROHRABACHER. That is correct. So we will find out. I will look into it. The group that did it was al-Nusrah.

Mr. KATZ. Okay. Then that makes sense, yes.

Mr. ROHRABACHER. And al-Nusrah, to you, is a radical Islamic group?

Mr. KATZ. Of course, it is a radical Islamic group.

Mr. ROHRABACHER. Okay. Yeah. Okay.

Mr. KATZ. Uh-huh.

Mr. ROHRABACHER. Okay. So doesn't that go a little bit contrary to what you were testifying?

Mr. KATZ. Well, if the focus is on ISIS per se, I think one thing that we know is that they are more radical even than al-Nusrah. In other words, there has been competition between the al-Nusrah Front and ISIS. I am not saying that it is better that al-Nusrah Front has made these advances, but what I think is that what we are seeing is that, as the Assad regime weakens, then eventually we are going to see a conflict between al-Nusrah and ISIS. In other words, they are not going to kiss and make up because they are both radicals.

Mr. ROHRABACHER. Right. Okay.

Mr. KATZ. That there is going to be a conflict between them.

Mr. ROHRABACHER. Well, with that, and Mr. Sires, and then I will have some other questions later.

Mr. SIRES. Thank you, Mr. Chairman.

You know, as I listened to your statements, I couldn't help but be a little bit confused in everything that was said here.

First, let me make an observation. You know, for the last few weeks we have been hearing about how the Syrian army has been weakened and how it looked like there was going to be defections and everything else. I really think that was a setup so that the Russians should come in and step in there in Syria. And now, today, I understand that the Russians bombed the Free—I wrote it down here—the Free Syrian Army post, but that wasn't ISIL.

So what does all of that mean? I mean, I assume that they were there to fight ISIL. Anybody? I guess I will get all three of your opinions since they were so diverse when you first gave your statements.

We will start with you.

Mr. KATZ. Okay. Yes. I think that in today's Washington Post, we have seen reports in which the Russians have claimed that they have made an attack on ISIS, but that opposition leader Hisham Marwah claimed that the Russian air strikes targeted civilians, not ISIS, killing 37 people in Homs. " 'The people of this area are opposed to ISIS,' said Marwah, vice president of the Syrian National Coalition, speaking by telephone from the U.S." His accounts, of course, couldn't be independently verified.

And so I think that this is the heart of the matter, that Putin claims he is there to fight ISIS, but what he is really there to do is to protect the Assad regime—protect the Assad regime against both the forces that oppose him most strongly, and this isn't ISIS. In other words, he is going to hit whoever is threatening Assad. He is not going to punctiliously avoid those forces that are not ISIS but which are threatening Assad. No. He wants to get rid of all the opposition to Assad.

Mr. SIRES. Dr. Aron.

Mr. ARON. As I said before in answer to Mr. Chairman's question, Putin is there to show that Russia does not abandon its allies.

Mr. SIRES. So in complete contrast to what people are claiming about us?

Mr. ARON. Make your own conclusions.

Mr. SIRES. No, I am just saying.

Mr. ARON. Yeah. And I think Putin—well, and I think Putin— you know, that point does not escape Putin, definitely. Well, you notice that immediately, you know, almost coincidental, Iraq now is cooperating with Russia on intelligence matters, and we are now worried what secrets is our Iraqi, I guess, allies are going to give Russia. It was a headline today.

So Putin is there to show that Russia does not abandon its allies. On a more strategic level, if I may reiterate, it is for Putin to regain a very important geopolitical asset. Russia is back in the Middle East after Sadat threw the Soviet Union out in 1972. Russia is back.

And, finally, it is an extremely important domestic political imperative for him to show that, whatever economic difficulties they have, Russia is a great power again, whether it is in Ukraine, whether it is in the Middle East, and God knows what is going to be next.

So these, to me, I think, is how Putin calculates it. Frankly, you know, so long as the regime that he supports is in power, I think that is Putin's strategic goal. Who he has to bomb along the way is, you know, I think is a secondary matter to him. He leaves it to the people on the ground.

Mr. SIRES. What do you think?

Mr. SARADZHYAN. Well, I haven't seen reports of what Russian warplanes have bombed what. My understanding is that Russia's interests in Syria require that Russia has a say in the future of this country. But the notion that Russia would bomb any of Assad's opponents, I think, is mistaken. Russia has hosted negotiations between some members of the Syrian opposition and Syrian officials. Russia has discussed, according to those opposition members, as cited in the press, potential participation of these opponents in the future government.

So, therefore, I think, as long as Russia's interest in Syria are honored, which is the presence of the Russian Navy in the Tartus, at the Tartus facility, continuing military industrial cooperation with Syria, and ensuring that there's no failed state in Syria, which is the largest concern of Russia, it would be open to accommodating a potential transition to a coalition government in the long run. Again, I haven't seen what they have bombed.

Mr. SIRES. But a coalition government, though, that would be in favor of Russia?

Mr. SARADZHYAN. That would take into account—it is not black and white—that would take into account Russia's interests, which include ensuring stability of Syria so that it doesn't become a failed state and, therefore, does not become a haven for terrorist groups that would then attack Russia and its allies, ensuring that Russia's naval presence remains in Syria, as it has been, and ensuring that Russia continues to trade with Syria in goods that let Russia diversify its economy, which is mostly about oil and gas. Syria is a major buyer of Russian machinery, including arms.

So as long as those interests are honored, Russia will remain open to the real dialogue, and the notion that it would bomb any of Assad's opponents, I think, is mistaken. If you read what the spokesperson for the Foreign Ministry said, Maria Zakharova, she said openly what has been said privately by Russian officials for a long time, that Russia is not married to the idea of keeping Assad necessarily in power.

Mr. SIRES. Okay. Somebody talk a little bit about the challenges that the Russians' military presence in Syria poses to the United States in terms of its conflict in Syria. What challenges do you see for us there?

Mr. KATZ. Well, clearly, if, in fact, the U.S. has its own bombing campaign against ISIS—and, certainly, Russia has its bombing campaign too—then I think the main question is deconfliction. We want to make sure that the two air forces don't run into each other. And so this is a serious issue, it seems to me.

On the other hand, other than that, I am not sure that the Russian military presence can really be seen as a threat to the United States. You know, Russia has fewer troops in Syria than we now have in Iraq. And so it strikes me that with our presence in Iraq, we are not exactly able to defeat ISIS with that. I don't think that what Russian presence we have seen in Syria is going to enable Russia to defeat ISIS if, in fact, that is what it wants to do. I think that, at best, what they are there to do is to bolster the Assad regime.

I have to disagree with my colleague about who Russia is or is not willing to bomb. I think that Russia is there to help the Assad regime. The Assad regime has certain very urgent opponents, and therefore I think that if that is what is necessary to attack, then that is what they will attack. I don't think Russia wants to get deeply involved in Syria, and in that caseI think thatPutin may have bitten off a little more than he can chew.

I have heard certain people from the Pentagon indicate that the U.S. can live with a Russian naval facility on the coast of Syria. It doesn't really threaten us very much. SoI don't think that we are necessarily opposed to Russia having normal relations, even favored relations with Syria.

And I think that at the beginning of the Syrian conflict our thought was that, well just as Moscow complained that after Assad Russia wouldn't have any influence in Iraq because the Iraqi Government would be pro-American, and what we have seen is increasing cooperation between Iraq and Russia. I think what we expected was that with the change of regime in Syria, which of course didn't happen, was that the new Syrian Government would eventually, after a certain pause, restore relations with Russia as well. But, of course, this is not what has happened.

Mr. SIRES. Dr. Aron, what challenges do you think it poses to——

Mr. ARON. No comment on that. You know, I thought that the actual topic, the threat of Islamic extremism in Russia, I think Syria does enter this simply because Syria has become a training ground for the jihadists from Central Asia, North Caucasus. But my point was that I think we may be seeing something much more threatening, and that is the Russian Muslim minorities inside Russia are beginning to go that route. They have very significant presence already in the troops of the jihadists in Syria.

And, frankly, if we thought that the Chechenswere a problem, there are 1 million of them, and there are 6½ million of Tatars and Bashkirs, and there are another 5 to 6 million inside Russia, including 2½ million migrants from Central Asia, who are constantly going back and forth, and Central Asia is completely now penetrated by ISIS recruiters and ISIS propaganda.

So talking of danger to the United States, those things are very rarely contained within national borders. So this, to me, is one of the offshoots. Regardless of what Putin does and what we do, I think that train is already in motion.

Mr. SIRES. And do you agree or disagree?

Mr. SARADZHYAN. Well, I agree. And as I said in my recent statement, the primary threat that emanates from that area is not whether Assad stays for a bit longer or is ousted now. It is whether this threat of violent jihadists can be contained and eliminated.

Mr. SIRES. So you don't think it poses any challenges to our efforts in Syria?

Mr. SARADZHYAN. I think whoever does anything, if it focuses on violent extremists and violent Islamists in Syria and Iraq, whoever goes after them, it is in the interests of the United States and it doesn't pose a threat, just like it is in the interests of Russia.

Mr. SIRES. Thank you, Mr. Chairman.

Mr. ROHRABACHER. Well, thank you very much.

We are going to have another series, which gives me an excuse to be able to ask some questions as well. And if you would like to ask some more, we will get that in as well.

I would like to place in the record a letter from John Quincy Adams to his fellows about his observations about Russia even as far back as John Quincy Adams, who, I believe, was our first Ambassador to Russia.

And he pointed out in his letter and lengthy analysis that the Russian character had been developed in great part due to its constant fight with Islam on its borders, that the Russia character of actually—and their national spirit—had been brought about by this fact that Islam was in a time of expansion, and Russia and the Russian people bore the brunt of that.

Thus, the idea that something could happen in the Islamic world that would be a great threat to Russians is something that is not just what Putin believes, but something that is engrained in Russian people, who over the years have had tragic incidences with, for example, a school in Beslan. And I went to that area to see that school and to talk to the local people. And they end up with hundreds of their children being murdered, basically. But that is not only. But you go through the years, this has been part of Russia's psyche.

I don't think—look, is there something—I don't think there is anything wrong with a country being led by a ruler who wants their country to be a great country. And I heard Mr. Putin's remarks to the United Nations, and he readily admitted that Russia had discarded the Soviet Union, and this was a new situation, and they are back to what normal countries should be judged by, not by standards that were established during the Cold War when Russia, itself, was being directed by an ideological, zealous clique in the Communist Party, the same way radical Islam is having such a major impact on Islam. The radical Islamists have that type of ability to impact on policies and large numbers of people through their violence.

So I really reject the idea that, well, Putin is only down there and the Russians are only down there to help Assad, their friend, although part of being a great country is making sure that when you make a deal with somebody that you keep the deal even when it gets tough and you don't leave your friends in the lurch after they have risked everything for you. And it seems that in the last few years the United States, as my colleague accidentally indicated, the United States——

Mr. SIRES. Some people.

Mr. ROHRABACHER. Yeah, well, we have left a lot of people behind here. And also, the United States policy was what? We had to get rid of Saddam Hussein. We felt compelled to go in and get Saddam Hussein. And now we feel compelled to make sure that Assad in some way doesn't hold power.

I don't get that. I think it was a mistake on our part. And I voted for that to support President Bush when he went into Iraq. That was a horrible mistake. And Saddam Hussein was not our enemy. And guess what, I don't think Assad is our enemy.

And if Russia is indeed there simply to help Assad—and what might happen to Syria, even if Assad is overthrown with non-ISIL forces—I don't think that it was the radicals that necessarily overthrew Qadhafi, but when the moderates overthrew Qadhafi with our help, we ended up with half of Libya now being controlled by radical Islam and a threat to the stability of the whole region.

Maybe Assad is like that. Maybe, no matter who overthrows him, as Mr. Putin was mentioning in his remarks at the U.N., that maybe this will create an unintended consequence of total catastrophe, not just Assad being overthrown by someone who isn't radical, but by the fact that you have a power vacuum then and chaos that will be exploited by these radical forces that are clearly present in that region.

So I personally, number one, think that we ought to start analyzing Russia, which is one of the reasons why you have this hearing, make sure that we understand what motives are going on here. And I don't think it is the motive that we had the same motive that when Khrushchev put the missiles into Cuba. I don't think that is the type of attitude that we are facing in the world today. And that is a lot different and that deserved the outrage that we had at that time.

But Assad being helped by Russia in the face of this type of turmoil, I don't see that this should be on our list of things to thwart, and it seems that our government is.

Back to the actual nature of Russia and radical Islam. Do you think, with all of the testimony we have heard today, I mean, it seems to me that wouldn't a government of Russia be justified in being concerned to hear that there are 5,000 Russian people who might at the end of this come back home and start committing the types of terrorism that is being experienced in different parts of the world? Isn't that a justified fear? Okay, please feel free to comment. Whatever.

Mr. ARON. Of course it is. And the fact that the Russian language is now the third most popular and that, you know, I have all kinds of stuff that you cannot fit in 5 minutes, but, you know, there have been reports that there were graffiti in Russian in Syria which read, ''Putin, we will pray in your palace,'' or through ''Tajikistan to Russia,'' which was one of the slogans of several groups. There is the Islamic Movement of Uzbekistan. I mean, this is a very vulnerable area.

Mr. ROHRABACHER. Yeah, a Tajik city was just taken over by the Taliban. Now, by the way, it is not that somebody is worried about that Russia will fall to these radicals. The issue is whether or not, because these radicals feel that they are now motivated and backed and have experience, that they might go into that country and start killing people in large numbers, whether it is herding a bunch of kids into a school and surrounding them with explosives, or whether it is setting off the type of explosions and things that we have seen in railroad cars in Western Europe.

There are fewer Muslims in Western Europe than what we have in Russia, and they are suffering from attacks, terrorist attacks there.

So, again, I think that the threat to Western civilization, to the non-Muslim world from radical Islam, Islamic terrorists, is real, and it makes sense if someone is also a target for that, that we don't try to do everything we can to undermine their efforts, but instead at least try to find ways to cooperate. That is what this hearing is all about.

And my colleague will now have his questions.

Mr. SIRES. Okay. Are you going to put that letter for the record?

Mr. ROHRABACHER. It is for the record.

Mr. SIRES. Okay.

I am trying to associate the Ukraine with what is going on in Syria. And do you think it has anything to do with Putin's decision to go into Syria, the fact that now there is like a stalemate there?

Mr. ARON. Well, one of the most interesting reactions that I heard from the—or read in the Russian media immediately after, because it was a surprise to everybody, part of the issue with Russia is that Putin literally is his own defense council, which is very difficult. It is a very dangerous situation. Crimea was a surprise to his ministers, to his closest aides, and so was Syria.

So the reaction from the Russian analysts was—one of the reactions—and remember I mentioned to you that there is a domestic political dimension to this, that is that Putin is popular not because of the Russian economy anymore. He used to be popular because they grew 7, 8 percent every year between 2000–2008. He is popular because he embodies this dream of Russia becoming a superpower like the Soviet Union used to be.

Mr. ROHRABACHER. That is called patriotism, right?

Mr. ARON. Well, we all want our countries to be great. The question is how we achieve it. That is a separate issue.

Mr. SIRES. We call it something else.

Mr. ARON. But the bottom line is, some of the analysts, some of the most respected Russian analysts, independent Russian analysts, said one of the reasons, not the whole reason, but one of the reasons to go to Syria is that Ukraine no longer generates enough of this patriotic heat that makes not all Russians, but quite a few to forget about the economic hardships, the 15 percent inflation, that the economy is probably going to shrink 5 to 6 percent this year, that there is unemployment, that the pensions are growing smaller and smaller due to inflation, that food products are now 15, 20, 30 percent more than they used to be because of the ban on the imports, and because there is no import substitution anymore. So all of those——

Mr. SIRES. The price of oil has gone down.

Mr. ARON. The price of oil is down. The ruble lost half of its value. But you see the headlines. We are in Syria now. We are present. They listen to us. They are afraid of us. They respect us. This is all very important.

And this is, you know, answering your question, this could have been one of the motivations. And you said, what is the connection to Ukraine? And I could talk to Ukraine for a long time. It is a very interesting subject. But for whatever reason, Putin now put Ukraine on hold. I don't think it is forever. I think he is going to return to that issue.

But there is something else now. He is like that man on the bicycle. I mean, that thing that, you know, when you put all your eggs in this what I call patriotic mobilization, you have got to give people, you know, fresh meat. You know, you are riding the tiger which is great, but the tiger requires fresh meat and bloody meat every now and then. So Ukraine is on hold, but Syria is in the headlines.

Mr. SIRES. Anybody else want to take a crack at that?

Mr. KATZ. Thank you.

Yes, I think in addition to what Dr. Aron had to say about the domestic political aspect of this and the link between Ukraine and Syria, I think there is also an important aspect in terms of relations with the West. In other words, the sanctions that the West has imposed on Russia as a result of actions in Ukraine are hurting the Russian economy, hurting it pretty badly. And I think that for Putin in particular, by making this argument that we can work together in Syria against ISIS, that this is a way sort of to restore relations with the West.

And to some extent I think we have seen it starting to work. President Francois Hollande actually came out and said maybe we should reduce the sanctions on Russia now that we have to deal with Syria together. Obviously, this is what he wants, although I did notice that most recently Francois Hollande indicated that what he wants to see is Russian actions against ISIS, not just words about it.

And of course Putin is taking advantage of the migration crisis. In other words, I think for a lot of Europeans in the European public, when it comes down to it, which is more important to them? Is it the migration crisis or what is happening in Ukraine? It is the migration crisis and if Putin is going to provide a way out of this, but the question is can he.

I would like to just also get back to an important point that Congressman Rohrabacher indicated, in other words, that in addition to the geopolitical competition between the U.S. and Russia, there is a basic philosophical difference about how to deal with Syria. The Russian argument is that Assad, as bad as he is, is less worse than ISIS, therefore we should support Assad. The Obama administration's argument is that ISIS is so awful that he has contributed to the rise of ISIS.

And the real trouble, I think, is that both might be right. In other words, that both arguments have a degree of validity. And what that implies is that, whether Assad goes or stays, ISIS is going to be a problem. And that is the situation, I think, that we are really stuck in, that we can argue about how to deal with the Syrian situation, but the real bottom line is that neither we nor the Russians really have an adequate response to this, that it has gotten out of hand, and whatever which way we go, it is going to remain a problem.

Mr. SIRES. Thank you, Mr. Chairman.

Mr. ROHRABACHER. Let's give our panelists each 1 minute to summarize what they would like to summarize on the issue, but 1 minute. And then the chairman, with his prerogative, will have a final statement as well. Then you can go.

Dr. Aron, do you want to give us 1 minute?

Mr. ARON. Yes, 1 minute is enough. I think, if indeed—and of course I gave you the tip of the iceberg on the evidence—if indeed we are witnessing a tipping point at which fundamentalist militant Islam is migrating from North Caucasus into Russia itself, I think this is a huge threat to Russia and the world.

In addition to that, these types of things usually are enhanced by domestic political crises and pressures. And Russia is in a very precarious state economically, politically, even though Putin would not admit it. There are all kinds of strains. And I think, while we are worried about the failed state in Syria, I think we should also worry about how the terrorism could become an issue for Russia and us.

Mr. ROHRABACHER. All right.

Mr. SARADZHYAN. I would like to reiterate that U.S. and Russia share common interests in countering terrorism and proliferation threats that emanate from Syria and Iraq, meaning terrorist groups based there. And I think regardless of disagreements on the future of Assad, both countries can and should work together to counter that threat, which is much more threatening, much more superior than intricacies of transition in Syria.

Thank you.

Mr. ROHRABACHER. Dr. Katz.

Mr. KATZ. The rise of jihadism in Russia is obviously not in Moscow's interest and it is not in the interest of America and the West either. But this rise of jihadism in Russia just isn't occurring in a void. The real tragic situation is that Russia's Muslims are not treated very well by the Russian Government, by Russian society.

And I think part of the problem that we face in dealing with this issue is that we can't either force or convince Vladimir Putin to treat his Muslims nicely. And that, I think, is the heart of the problem: That the Muslim issue in Russia is not one that America is in a position to address. Only Moscow can do that, and at the moment it doesn't want to do so very effectively.

Mr. ROHRABACHER. Well, thank you all for joining us today. Just a few short thoughts, and that is, let us remember that when Saddam Hussein was eliminated it brought chaos. When Qadhafi was eliminated it brought chaos. There were alternatives there, you know, Qadhafi in particular, but also with Saddam Hussein.

And we were told that this third force was our alternative to Assad. And I think the Russians are very concerned that even if Assad is eliminated by this third force, even if that is the case, you are going to have just what happened in these other countries—chaos, which is then exploited by the most radical Islamic forces within those societies.

And what would that impact on Russia, which we described today? This is a greater concern than actually is in Western Europe. And we can see what is going on, the frantic way Western Europe is dealing with radical Islam and the impact of it.

President Putin just gave—not just, several months ago, I think it must have been 6 months to a year ago now—went down and provided President el-Sisi of Egypt $2 billion worth of credit—$2 billion—even at a time in which we have had testimony of a weakness in the economy of Russia. Now, why did that happen? Is that just because he wants Russia to dominate Egypt?

Listen, Russia is a—like England and other great countries in the world, in China, in Japan, in India, and these countries—these are great countries of the world that their leaders calculate what is good for their country. And in the long run, I believe the reason why that $2 billion and that help to General el-Sisi was coming forward was because Putin acknowledges that if radical Islam were to take over in Egypt, that these other countries would be swept away in the Gulf and you would have radical Islam pouring into Central Asia, and that would dramatically impact the security of his country and the future of the world.

And I think that there is some strategic thinking going on rather than simply he is a tough guy showing his muscles to the world and he is a gangster thug, which is usually the answers you get when you are trying to come up with a real analysis of what the hell is going on with Russia and these various parts of the world.

So with that said, I think we need, I think the United States needs to cooperate with people who are going to help us defeat radical Islamic terrorism, whether it is Putin, or whether it is Assad, or whether who that is, because those people, especially, have the United States in target for their terrorism.

If a nuclear bomb goes off from a terrorist group in the United States, it won't be from Russia, it won't be from Assad, it won't be probably from Japan or any of these other countries. It will be from radical Islamic terrorists. And if we are going to protect our people, we have got to be rational and we have got to reach out to those people who are the enemy of our enemy. And I buy that formula, and I think it will make us safer.

And with that said, I appreciate the insights that this panel has given us today in understanding the world and having some good thoughts about what strategies we can use.

So this hearing is now adjourned.

[Whereupon, at 3:54 p.m., the subcommittee was adjourned.]

APPENDIX

MATERIAL SUBMITTED FOR THE RECORD

SUBCOMMITTEE HEARING NOTICE
COMMITTEE ON FOREIGN AFFAIRS
U.S. HOUSE OF REPRESENTATIVES
WASHINGTON, D.C. 20515-6128

Subcommittee on Europe, Eurasia, and Emerging Threats
Dana Rohrabacher (R-CA), Chairman

September 28, 2015

TO: MEMBERS OF THE COMMITTEE ON FOREIGN AFFAIRS

You are respectfully requested to attend an OPEN hearing of the Committee on Foreign Affairs, to be held by the Subcommittee on Europe, Eurasia, and Emerging Threats in Room 2200 of the Rayburn House Office Building (and available on the Committee website at www.foreignaffairs.gov):

DATE: Wednesday, September 30, 2015

TIME: 2:00 p.m.

SUBJECT: The Threat of Islamist Extremism in Russia

WITNESSES: Leon Aron, Ph.D.
Resident Scholar and Director of Russian Studies
The American Enterprise Institute

Mr. Simon Saradzhyan
Assistant Director
U.S.-Russia Initiative to Prevent Nuclear Terrorism
Belfer Center for Science and International Affairs
Harvard University

Mark N. Katz, Ph.D.
Professor of Government and Politics
School of Policy, Government, and International Affairs
George Mason University

By Direction of the Chairman

COMMITTEE ON FOREIGN AFFAIRS

MINUTES OF SUBCOMMITTEE ON _____ *Europe, Eurasia, and Emerging Threats* _____ HEARING

Day___*Wednesday*___Date___*September 30, 2015*___Room_____*2200*_____

Starting Time ____*2:00 pm*____Ending Time ____*3:54 pm*____

Recesses ___*1*___ (*2:38 pm* to *3:11 pm*) (____to____) (____to____) (____to____) (____to____) (____to____)

Presiding Member(s)

Rep. Rohrabacher

Check all of the following that apply:

Open Session ☑   Electronically Recorded (taped) ☑
Executive (closed) Session ☐   Stenographic Record ☑
Televised ☐

TITLE OF HEARING:

The Threat of Islamic Extremism in Russia

SUBCOMMITTEE MEMBERS PRESENT:

Rep. Sires

NON-SUBCOMMITTEE MEMBERS PRESENT: *(Mark with an * if they are not members of full committee.)*

Rep. Weber

HEARING WITNESSES: Same as meeting notice attached? Yes ☑ No ☐
(If "no", please list below and include title, agency, department, or organization.)

STATEMENTS FOR THE RECORD: *(List any statements submitted for the record.)*

TIME SCHEDULED TO RECONVENE _____
or
TIME ADJOURNED ____*3:54 pm*____

Subcommittee Staff Director